▶ Presented to ◀

By

Date

Occasion

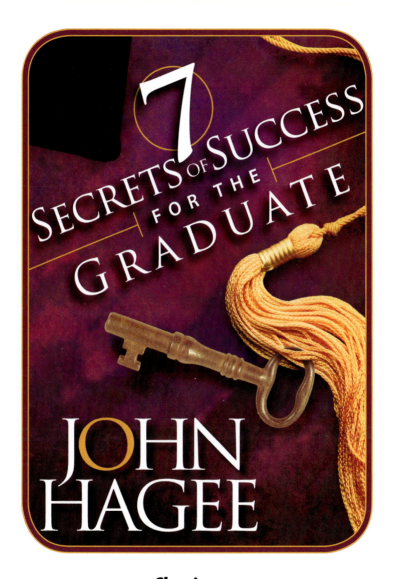

7 SECRETS OF SUCCESS FOR THE GRADUATE

JOHN HAGEE

Charisma
HOUSE
A STRANG COMPANY

Most Strang Communications/Charisma House/Siloam/FrontLine/Realms products are available at special quantity discounts for bulk purchase for sales promotions, premiums, fund-raising, and educational needs. For details, write Strang Communications/Charisma House/Siloam/FrontLine/Realms, 600 Rinehart Road, Lake Mary, Florida 32746, or telephone (407) 333-0600.

7 Secrets of Success for the Graduate by John Hagee
Published by Charisma House
A Strang Company
600 Rinehart Road
Lake Mary, Florida 32746
www.charismahouse.com

Unless otherwise indicated, Scripture quotations are from The Holy Bible, English Standard Version, copyright © 2001 by Crossway Bibles, a division of Good News Publishers. Used by permission.

Scripture quotations marked cev are from the Contemporary English Version. Copyright © 1991, 1992, 1995 by American Bible Society. Used by permission.

Scripture quotations marked nkjv are taken from the New King James Version. Copyright © 1982 by Thomas Nelson, Inc. Used by permission. All rights reserved.

Scripture quotations marked nlt are taken from The Holy Bible, New Living Translation, copyright © 1996, 2004. Used by permission of Tyndale House Publishers, Inc., Wheaton, Illinois, 60189.

Scripture quotations marked The Message are from *The Message: The Bible in Contemporary English*, copyright © 1993, 1994, 1995, 1996, 2000, 2001, 2002. Used by permission of NavPress Publishing Group. All rights reserved.

Cover design by Rachel Campbell

Library of Congress Control Number: 2006934404
International Standard Book Number: 978-1-59979-061-9

07 08 09 10 11 — 987654321
Printed in the United States of America

▶Contents . . .

WHAT SUCCESS IS NOT

*THE PRE-SECRET

If you believe you can succeed—or you believe you can't—guess what?

You're right!

You are **UNIQUE**. When you were born, the genius of God exploded and made a person that the world

HAS NEVER SEEN BEFORE

and will never see again. You were born to do good. You were born to succeed. You were born to bless the lives of others.

YOU HAVE UNLIMITED POTENTIAL, BUT YOU MUST LEARN HOW TO RELEASE IT TO REACH YOUR DESTINY.

But before you can really understand what success is, it first helps to **UNDERSTAND** what success *is not*.

#1 SUCCESS <u>is not</u> Money

If you think success is money, consider these facts of life:

▶ **Money can buy** you a palace of breath-taking splendor, but money cannot buy you the love and respect of the people who live in it.

▶ **Money can buy** the finest physicians in an hour of sickness, but money cannot buy the God-given gift of health.

▶ **Money can buy** you a bed of solid gold, but money cannot buy you one minute of rest or inner peace.

▶ **Money will attract** legions of people to you, but money cannot buy you the treasure of one true friend.

▶ **Money can buy** a church pew with your name engraved on it in gold script, but money will not buy you a ticket to heaven or a pure heart.

Those who love money will never have enough. How meaningless to think that wealth brings true happiness!

—SOLOMON

the wisest man who has ever lived

and richest king of Israel

ECCLESIASTES 5:10, NLT

#2 SUCCESS <u>is not</u> REACHING A GOAL

Motivational speaker and minister Bob Harrison says, **"SETTING GOALS IS THE MOST DANGEROUS THING A PERSON CAN DO."** Why? Because once you set a goal in one area, you take attention away from all others.

Too often the woman who sets out to be a vice president by age thirty-five is a divorcée by twenty-nine, or the fellow who sets out to be a pop star will make compromises that will plague his spirit the rest of his life. You may attain your goal but at the same time lose everything worth living for.

It is not that goals are evil, but **THEY MUST BE BALANCED**—you must also realize that attaining one goal is only a small step toward achieving more important things. When goals became gods, they become ends in themselves. Reaching a goal can destroy you by the temptation to stagnate and the illusion of accomplishment, if you don't have a larger purpose beyond it. **GOALS MUST BE TARGETS** and not terminal destinations.

Life's most important revelation is that the journey means more than the destination.

#3 SUCCESS is not Power

SADDAM HUSSEIN ruled Iraq for decades with an iron fist. He had the power of life and death over millions of Iraqis; he amassed a fortune of billions; he built a series of elaborate mansions for himself and members of his family while the children of Iraq starved. He had absolute power, but Saddam Hussein was not successful. His reign of terror is now over, extinguished through the courageous leadership of President George W. Bush and the heroics of America's armed forces.

Long ago, **THE APOSTLE PAUL** stood, bound in chains before Felix, a Roman governor. Paul reasoned with Felix about the "righteousness and . . . the coming judgment" (Acts 24:25). The Bible records that Felix shook so violently he could hardly remain sitting on his throne. He had the power of the Roman Empire behind him, yet he shook before a prisoner in chains.

Yes, Felix had power, but power is not success. Two thousand years later we call our sons "Paul" and our cats "Felix."

SUCCESS IS NOT POWER.

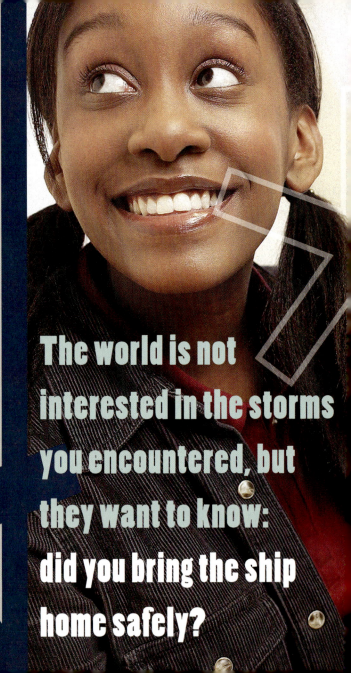

The world is not interested in the storms you encountered, but they want to know: did you bring the ship home safely?

#4 SUCCESS is not Having it ALL

LEO TOLSTOY tells the story of a rich man who always wanted more. One day he heard that for a thousand rubles he could have all the land he was able to walk around in a single day, as long as he returned to the starting point by sundown. If not, he would forfeit it all.

So the man rose early and set out. He kept pushing himself to go further and further. Suddenly he realized it was mid-afternoon and he would have to travel very fast if he were to return in time to claim the land.

As the sun got lower in the sky, he began to run. Coming within sight of his starting point, he exerted his last ounce of energy, plunged over the finish line, collapsed, and died. His servant dug a grave and buried him on the spot.

The title of this story is **"HOW MUCH LAND DOES A MAN NEED?"** Tolstoy concluded by saying, "Six feet from his head to his heels was all he needed." You can't get it all or keep it all. Success is *not* having it all.

> To reach the port of success we must sail, sometimes with the wind and sometimes against it—but we must sail, not drift or lie at anchor.
> **—Oliver Wendell Holmes**

#5 SUCCESS is not Determined by Your CIRCUMSTANCES

Success is not found in your circumstance.

Success is overcoming your circumstance.

HELEN KELLER was born blind and deaf, yet she graduated from college with honors. **MARGARET THATCHER**, England's first—and only—woman prime minister who joined with President Ronald Reagan to crush Communism and bring down the Berlin Wall, lived upstairs over her father's small grocery store. For a while her childhood home had no running water or indoor plumbing. **MICHAEL JORDAN**, who is doubtless the greatest basketball player to ever walk on the court, was cut from his high school team. **BILL GATES**, the billionaire who founded Microsoft, was a college dropout. **GOLDA MEIER**, Israel's first—and only—woman prime minister, was a divorced grandmother from Milwaukee.

SUCCESS IS NOT DETERMINED BY YOUR CIRCUMSTANCES.

Success is not an event; it's a lifelong journey. You cannot possess what you are unwilling to pursue. Success comes to those who plan, to those who prepare, to those who are persistent, and to those who are willing to endure pain TO ACHIEVE THEIR GOALS.

#6 SUCCESS is not Maintaining the STATUS QUO

> There is no poverty that can overcome diligence. —Japanese Proverb

Not long ago, **FUJIO CHO**, Toyota Motor Corporation's president, announced that a new $800 million factory would be built in our city of San Antonio. During the announcement, he said, "There is an important word in the Toyota vocabulary that you'll hear a lot in coming years—*kaizen*." *Kaizen* means **"CONTINUOUS IMPROVEMENT."**

I was born in 1940, and I remember that after WWII, the words *made in Japan* were synonymous with questionable workmanship. Today when I go to the mall to shop with my wife, I do not see the Hudsons, Studebakers, Nashes, Kaisers, and Packards I saw in parking lots as a child, I see Nissans, Toyotas, Hondas, Isuzus, and Subarus.

#7 SUCCESS <u>is not</u> Avoiding CRITICISM

Success is not avoiding criticism, because this is impossible. Success is learning how to receive criticism without fear as you replace your **DEFENSE MECHANISM** with honesty, love, forgiveness, and a sense of humor.

The trouble with most of us is that we would rather be ruined by praise than saved by criticism.

There are three ways to avoid criticism:

1. Do nothing!
2. Be nothing!
3. Say nothing!

There are two kinds of criticism: justified and unjustified. How do you tell the difference? Criticism that is justified has at least a measure of truth in it. **AN ARAB PROVERB** states, "If one person calls you a donkey, forget it. If five people call you a donkey, buy a saddle."

Be discerning, and **LEARN TO GROW** from what others say to you. Success is not avoiding criticism; it very much demands the opposite.

THE POWER
of Seven

THE PRE-SECRET

I have been a scholar of the Word of God for many years and have been especially attracted to the study of biblical numerology. **THERE'S A MESSAGE** in Bible numerology, just as there is in the written Word. The number seven, which is the number of perfection, is particularly interesting to me.

Throughout this book I will give you **SEVEN SECRETS FOR SUCCESS** that I have learned along the way. Within each secret are seven key truths that you can apply in your life. As you read each secret, I have included some important elements to help you hone your thoughts and goals. They are:

"The Key to Success": Here you can write down your plans to unlock the secret of the particular success discussed.

Journal pages: This is "your space" to jot down thoughts and ideas, and have friends and family write down their words of advice to you.

FAQs: OK, so maybe they're not your frequently asked questions, but this section was designed to help you dig into the recesses of your mind a little deeper.

I pray that these truths will produce a prosperous harvest above and **BEYOND YOUR WILDEST DREAMS**.

I BELIEVE SUCCESS IS FOR YOU—*NOW*!

SECRET

1

MAXIMIZING THE POWER OF
YOUR MIND

Don't copy the behavior and customs of this world, but let God transform you into a new person by changing the way you think. Then you will learn to know God's will for you, which is good and pleasing and perfect. —PAUL

Romans 12:2, NLT

Everything can be taken from a man but one thing: the last of human free-doms, to choose one's attitude in any given set of circumstances, to choose one's own way.

—DR. VICTOR FRANKL (1905–1997)
WWII concentration camp survivor
and author of *Man's Search for Meaning*

16

WITHIN YOU is a kingdom of unlimited potential: **YOUR MIND.** Your ability to achieve staggering success or unspeakable disappointment depends on the choices made in your mind—and one choice in particular.

THAT SINGLE CHOICE DETERMINES YOUR JOY, your peace, the quality of your family life, your professional success, and most importantly, the destiny of your soul. That single **CHOICE** is made every hour of every day you live.

That single choice is *HOW YOU CHOOSE to react to what has been done to you in the past or is being done to you right now.*

Your attitude will determine your future.

PROFILE
of an Attitude

Let me give you my definition of an attitude in a series of four statements.

▶ Your attitude is an inward feeling expressed by outward behavior. Your attitude is **SEEN BY ALL** without you saying a word.

▶ Your attitude is the advance person of **YOUR TRUE SELF**. The roots of your attitude are hidden, but its fruit is always visible.

▶ Your attitude is your **BEST FRIEND** or your **WORST ENEMY**. It draws people to you or repels people from you.

▶ Your attitude determines the **QUALITY OF YOUR RELATIONSHIPS** with your employer, your friends, your boyfriend/girlfriend or spouse, your family, and God Almighty.

#1 Your ATTITUDE is a CHOICE

You choose your attitude every morning when you get up. If you woke up this morning and did not find your picture in the obituary column, get happy.

KING DAVID said, "This is the day the LORD has made; we will rejoice and be glad in it" (Ps. 118:24 NKJV). He chose to rejoice whether he felt like it or not—we need to do the same!

POLISH PIANIST PADEREWSKI was told by his teacher that his hands were too small to master the keyboard. Yet the fire in Paderewski's belly to become a celebrated pianist drove him to overcome this limitation. He became world-renowned.

When the great **ITALIAN TENOR ENRICO CARUSO** first began to study voice, he was told his voice sounded like the wind whistling through the window. Showing an attitude that conquered adversity, Caruso went on to became one of the world's greatest tenors ever.

You can't change the past, but you can choose to have an overcomer's attitude in facing the future. That attitude is the beginning of your success in every area.

#2 YOUR Attitude determines <u>your</u> ATTAINMENTS

Miracles come in "cans." You must choose an "*I can*" attitude if you are ever to accomplish what you are after.

Perhaps you're not reaching your objective because you lack motivation. You've tried and failed, so you've quit trying. **HAVE YOU REALLY TRIED YOUR BEST?** On your job? In your relationships? With your education? With your dreams? Why don't you try one more time? This time, purpose in your heart to give it all you've got.

STOP SAYING "IF" and start saying, "I can by God's grace."

STOP SAYING, "IT'S IMPOSSIBLE," and start saying, "With God all things are possible" (Matt. 19:26).

STOP SAYING, "I DON'T KNOW THE RIGHT PEOPLE," and start saying, "I know Almighty God, and through Him all things are possible."

STOP SAYING, "I'M NOT EDUCATED," and start saying: "If any of you lacks wisdom, let him ask God...and it will be given him" (James 1:5).

Your attitude **DETERMINES** your attainments.

Conquering your stress

#3 Your ATTITUDE Determines your Emotional and Physical HEALTH

Doctors are finding that **STRESS** is right up there with smoking on the list of risk factors for chronic disease. While we see antismoking campaigns everywhere, why don't we see any "antistressing out" programs?

It is really not stress that kills people, but how they handle it. To **LIVE STRESS-FREE** is to live accomplishment free. Without any pressure or adversity, a diamond would just be a lump of coal.

At a ski lodge I once saw a sign that read: "The man who can make me angry can kill me." When I asked about it, the owner told me the following story: "My brother-in-law was one of the most successful businessmen in Colorado. He had just purchased a brand-new Cadillac and had driven it less than one mile when someone hit him, denting the front fender. He got out of his car screaming like a madman. Suddenly he dropped dead in the middle of the street. From that day until this one, I have lived with that motto."

begins with YOUR attitude.

#4 YOUR Attitude Overcomes ADVERSITY

If what you're doing doesn't produce resistance, what you're doing is not worth doing. Consider these facts:

Without the resistance of water, ships can't float.
Without the resistance of air, planes can't fly.
Without the resistance of gravity, men can't walk.
A rubber band is effective only when it's stretched.
A turtle gets nowhere until it sticks its neck out.
Kites rise against the wind, not with the wind.

THE PROCESS OF STRUGGLE

develops your character, your strength, and your mind.

Stop hiding from success because you're afraid you'll fail. Failure is necessary. Stop fearing risk. Have faith in God, and step up to reach for the stars.

Everything in life involves **RISK**:
To laugh is to risk appearing the fool.
To weep is to risk appearing sentimental.
To reach out for another is to risk involvement.
To expose your feelings is to risk exposing your true self.
To share your ideas and dreams with others is to risk rejection.
To love another is to risk not being loved in return.
To live is to risk dying.
To hope is to risk despair.

TAKE A RISK! Climb out on the limb where the fruit is. Stop living life hugging the tree trunk and whining because other people get the fruit. Reach for the brass ring, and stand in the winner's circle.

Stop saying, "I could, *but*..."
Start saying, "Today I *will*..."

25

#5 YOUR Attitude Determines the Attitude of OTHERS

TEDDY ROOSEVELT, the twenty-sixth president of the United States, said, "The most important single ingredient in the formula of success is knowing how to get along with people."

JOHN D. ROCKEFELLER, one of the richest Americans, said, "The ability to deal with people is as purchasable a commodity as sugar or coffee, and I will pay more for that ability than any other under the sun."

JESUS CHRIST said, "Whatever you wish that others would do to you, do also to them" (Matt. 7:12).

I REPEAT: YOUR ATTITUDE TOWARD OTHERS DETERMINES THEIR ATTITUDE TOWARD YOU.

The Key to Success . . .

What I need to change most about my attitude

▶ _____

_____

_____

_____

_____

_____

_____

_____

_____

_____

_____

_____

_____

_____

_____

MIND POWER

#6 YOUR Attitude is CONTAGIOUS

Your attitude is contagious to your family, your church, and any business you're involved in.

Look around you! Analyze the conversations of people you know who lead unhappy, unfulfilled lives. They are the people who are too negative, too critical, and too argumentative. They are sarcastic and arrogant. They act like junkyard dogs from 9:00 until 5:00. They have mastered **THE ART OF CREATIVE SUFFERING**. They cannot keep friends, a job, or a spouse.

Hang around them too much, and you will soon be like them because attitudes are contagious. They breed confidence or despair.

Consider the battle of David and Goliath. When Goliath came against Israel, forty thousand Israeli soldiers thought, "He's so big we can never kill him." David looked at the same giant and thought, "He's so big I can't miss him."

Your attitude is a choice; your attitude determines your attainments; and your attitude overcomes adversity. Your attitude toward others also determines their attitude toward you. Your attitude is contagious.

Start each day saying:

I **CAN** do all things through Christ. —PHILIPPIANS 4:13, NKJV

All things **ARE** possible for one who believes. —MARK 9:23

Whatever things you ask in prayer, believing, **YOU WILL RECEIVE**. —MATTHEW 21:22, NKJV

In all these things we are **MORE THAN CONQUERORS** through him who loved us. —ROMANS 8:37

#7 YOUR Attitude <u>can</u> OVERCOME ANY Disability

Most people wait for their circumstances to change before they decide to change their attitude. That's backward. Look at the things people quit because of circumstances. They quit jobs and business ventures. They quit the church. They quit marriages. They quit college. They're waiting for something to change before they change. The truth is: **If you'll change the way you think about your world, your world will change today.**

Listen again to the words of the apostle Paul, "Keep your minds on whatever is true, pure, right, holy, friendly, and proper. Don't ever stop thinking about what is truly worthwhile and worthy of praise." (Phil. 4:8 CEV).

You are the absolute sovereign over a kingdom of unlimited resources—your mind. You and you alone determine your destiny by the choice of your attitudes.

FAQs

1. What are some of the things causing stress or grief in your life right now?

▶ _____

_____

_____

_____

2. What are you doing to handle them?

▶ _____

_____

_____

_____

3. How can you enlist God's supernatural help to keep a positive attitude?

▶ _____

_____

_____

_____

You must have the same attitude that Christ Jesus had.

—PAUL

Philippians 2:5, NLT

journal ▶

SECRET

2

CONQUERING THE QUIT FACTOR

Many of life's failures are individuals who did not realize how close they were to success when they gave up.

—JOHN HAGEE

Do you see what this means—all these pioneers who blazed the way, all these veterans cheering us on? It means we'd better get on with it. Strip down, start running— and never quit! No extra spiritual fat, no parasitic sins. Keep your eyes on Jesus, who both began and finished this race we're in.

—PAUL

Hebrews 12:1-2, THE MESSAGE

On my eighth birthday, my mother—who was the guiding light of my life—began to teach me a word that would forever shape my life. That word was **PERSEVERANCE**.

Her definition of *perseverance* was simple:

THOSE WHO PERSEVERE ARE THE ONES LEFT STANDING WHEN EVERYONE ELSE QUITS!

She would take her angelic hands, hold my face until her dark eyes penetrated my soul, and say, "**YOU ARE MY SON**, and quitting is unthinkable! You must learn that perseverance begins with perspiration."

#1

Perseverance
BEGINS <u>with</u> Perspiration

The difference between history's boldest accomplishments and its most staggering failures is simply the willingness to persevere.

"**TODAY**, I'm going to take you to Mr. Jodick's cotton farm and let you pick cotton," Mother stated.

I was delighted because the job paid money. I asked, "How much does this job pay?"

"**IT PAYS ONE DOLLAR** per hundred pounds picked—not pulled—picked! You can't pull the cotton boll; you can only pick the cotton out of the boll."

"**HOW LONG DOES IT TAKE** to pick one hundred pounds?" I asked. I was mentally calculating the fortune I was going to make.

"That depends on how hard you work!"

When we arrived, I jumped out of the car, and Mr. Jodick handed me a sixteen-foot cotton sack. When you're eight years old, a sixteen-foot cotton sack reaches from here to eternity.

Then came the real shock. Mr. Jodick took me to the row of cotton I was going to pick. The cotton was over my head! Each row was a thousand feet long, seemingly ending at the horizon. "How do

you get to the end of the row?" I asked.

"Heads down; hiney up!" he answered. "That means **START WORKING AND START SWEATING AND DON'T STOP UNTIL THE JOB IS FINISHED**." I worked in that cotton patch until cotton season was over. I earned twenty-three dollars.

I learned early on that perseverance begins with **PERSPIRATION.**

#2 PERSEVERANCE is Sustained by PURPOSE

Do you know your **DIVINE** purpose?

If not, you will live in a state of perpetual dissatisfaction until you clearly understand God's reason for putting you on this earth.

Saul was a **ZEALOUS PHARISEE** who ruthlessly persecuted the early church and tried to destroy it, but God's purpose for Saul's life was for him to preach the gospel of Jesus Christ to the Gentiles. God's purpose and Saul's passion collided on the road to Damascus. God slapped Saul from his horse, blinded him, and asked, "Saul, Saul, why are you persecuting me?" That encounter **CHANGED SAUL'S LIFE FOREVER**. Saul, the Pharisee, became Paul, the founder of the New Testament church. His divine purpose had been revealed to him.

I've met many very successful people who have reached their goals, but they have no peace, no joy, no sense of accomplishment. **WHY?** Because life without knowing one's divine purpose leads to disillusionment and emptiness.

Take time today to examine your life. If you are not controlled by the purpose of God, you are controlled by the world, the flesh, and perhaps Satan himself. **DETERMINE TO FIND GOD'S PURPOSE FOR CREATING YOU.** It is the only path to the fullest life you can hope to live.

#3 <u>the</u> Perseverance PRINCIPLE:

It's Always Too Soon to Quit

There comes a time in every life

when quitting looks good...
when problems seem
   insurmountable...
when giants seem unbeatable...
when mountains seem
   unmovable...
when defeat seems inescapable...
when retreat seems the only
   option!

But remember: It's **ALWAYS** too soon to quit!

I wish I had a dollar for every time my mother said, "**FINISH WHAT YOU START!**" She also said, "The very worst men are those who begin and then give up!"

The Bible does not say, "Those who begin well shall be saved;" it says, "The one who endures to the end will be **SAVED**" [Matt. 24:13].

Whatever you're going through today, keep trying. A mountain only seems high from the valley. The road to success runs **UPHILL**, so don't expect to break any speed records. The thing to do when all else fails is: begin again.

#4 PERSEVERANCE
Produces CHAMPIONS

WILMA RUDOLPH was born prematurely, the twentieth of twenty-two children, and she wasn't expected to live. A bout of **POLIO**, among other illnesses that affected her infancy, left her legs crooked and her feet twisted inward, resulting in her wearing leg braces for most of her childhood. Wilma, however, was determined to make a place for herself in the world without those braces.

When she was eleven, she walked into the doctor's office and told him, "I have something I'd like to share with you." She proceeded to take the **BRACES OFF** and walk across the office to where he was sitting.

"How long have you been doing this?" the doctor questioned.

"FOR THE PAST YEAR."

"Well, since you've been honest in sharing this with me," the doctor replied, "sometimes I'll let you take them off and walk around the house."

"SOMETIMES" was the only permission she needed. She never put those braces on again. That was only the beginning.

Moving on into middle school and high school, Wilma wanted not only to walk but also to **RUN AND JUMP** with the other kids. She convinced the basketball coach to give her ten minutes a day with the promise that if he did, "I will give you in return a world-class athlete." At first he laughed at the **SIX-FOOT, EIGHTY-NINE POUND STRAGGLER**, but in the end he agreed. The next year Wilma made the team.

With that same attitude and **PERSISTENCE**, Wilma kept working. When basketball season ended, she decided to try track. That's when she realized that she was fast. As a fourteen-year-old high school freshman, Wilma started to work out with a training team at the **UNIVERSITY OF TENNESSEE**.

The result of her persistence? In **1956**, she got a bronze medal in the Olympics as part of the women's 400-meter relay team, and in 1960 she became the first woman in history to win three gold medals in track and field. Through persistence, Wilma went from being a cripple to being **A CHAMPION**.

45

#5 Perseverance is the KEY to Perfection

PLATO wrote the first sentence of his famous *Republic* nine different ways before he was satisfied. **CICERO** practiced speaking before friends every day for thirty years to perfect his elocution. **NOAH WEBSTER** labored thirty-six years writing his dictionary, crossing the Atlantic twice to gather material.

MILTON rose at four in the morning every day in order to write *Paradise Lost*. **SIR WALTER SCOTT** put in fifteen hours a day at his desk, rising at four in the morning. He averaged writing a book every two months and turned out the Waverly novels at one a month. **VIRGIL** spent seven years on his *Georgics* and twelve on the *Aeneid*. Nevertheless, he was so displeased with the latter that he tried to rise from his deathbed to throw the manuscript into the flames. **BEETHOVEN** is unsurpassed in his painstaking fidelity to his music— nearly every bar of his was written and rewritten at least a dozen times.

MICHELANGELO's *Last Judgment*, one of the twelve master paintings of the ages, was the product of eight years of unremitting toil. Over two thousand studies of it were found among his papers. During his mighty labor in the Sistine Chapel he refused to have any communication with any person, even at his own house. He had to persist without interruption in producing exactly what was in his heart.

THROUGHOUT HISTORY, great men have known perseverance is the key to excellence.

Have you failed? In a relationship? In your work? In your education? God is the God of second chances. Try again! Don't give an alibi; **GIVE ANOTHER TRY**.

The Key to Success...

Things I will never give up on in my life

▶ _____

_____

_____

_____

_____

_____

_____

_____

_____

_____

_____

_____

QUIT FACTOR 2

#6 PERSEVERANCE is Part of the Christian LIFE

Hell has thrown the kitchen sink at me, and I'm still fighting the good fight. I'm still enduring! I'm still standing! I will not bend, bow, or burn! I will not look back, let up, slow down, back away, or be quiet. My past is forgiven; my present is redeemed; my future is secure. I no longer need position, prominence, or popularity. I don't have to be right, recognized, regarded, or rewarded.

I now live by faith and walk in divine anointing. My face is set; my gait is fast; my goal is heaven; my road is narrow; my way may be rough and my companions few. **I cannot be bought**, compromised, detoured, lured away, turned back, deluded, or delayed. **I will not flinch** in the face of sacrifice or hesitate in the presence of the adversary. The devil's mad, and I'm glad!

—2 CORINTHIANS 4:8–9, HIT

(Hagee International Translation)

#7 Perseverance is a DECISION

PERSEVERANCE is a decision! It's a decision that every winner makes, including gold medalists at the **OLYMPICS**. What magnificent bodies the runners have. They are the picture of power and strength. The marathon begins, and all run well at first. Then some begin to sweat. After several miles, exhaustion sets in. One gets weary and drops out. Another trips. Another faints. Another gasps for air and drops out.

Who is the winner? **THE ONE WHO ENDURES** to the end. The overcomer is the one who receives the crown.

All great living begins when you look into your soul and decide you will not play the role of a coward. You make a definite decision. **YOU WILL ENDURE**. You will persevere—period!

Be persistent! Never . . . never . . . **NEVER** give up! It's too soon to quit!

FAQs

1. What things in your life right now are worth not giving up on?

▶ _____

_____

_____

_____

2. Who is depending on you right now to persist? Who will be depending on you in the future?

▶ _____

_____

_____

_____

3. What things are in your heart that you feel God wants you to see through to the end?

▶ _____

_____

_____

_____

Committed and persistent work pays off.

—Proverbs 28:20, The Message

journal ▶

See yourself and others **as God sees**. When that happens, you will be poised instead of timid, enthusiastic instead of bored, **successful** instead of failing, energetic instead of fatigued, agreeable instead of cantankerous, positive **instead of negative**, self-forgiving instead of self-condemning, and **self-respecting** instead of self-disgusting.

—JOHN HAGEE

Love never fails.

—PAUL

1 Corinthians 13:8, NKJV

Jesus revealed this third secret in the **SECOND GREAT COMMANDMENT**, "You shall love your neighbor as yourself" (Matt. 22:39).

Notice that this scriptural truth has two parts: Love your neighbor; love yourself.

IF YOU DO NOT LIKE YOURSELF, YOU WILL NOT LIKE YOUR NEIGHBOR.

Clearly seeing the world around you can only be done **THROUGH THE EYES OF GOD'S LOVE**.

Realizing your goals and dreams begins with seeing yourself as God sees you. Rid yourself of **DOUBTS**; build self-confidence and self-worth. Learn that seeing yourself and your neighbor as God sees is **THE SECRET** to happiness in work, relationships, and everything you do.

#1 Love is PATIENT

How patient are you? Do you stand in front of the microwave oven screaming, "Hurry up"? Do you grow impatient brewing instant coffee? I know how you feel.

Yet love is patient. It endures. True love, God's kind of love, never gets tired of waiting. His love doesn't give up on an alcoholic or a drug addict. Patient love endures a loveless, seemingly lifeless marriage. Patient love locks its jaw and hangs on with undying hope for a better tomorrow.

Because love's foundation is faith in God, it never quits. It sees as God sees and knows there is always hope. It is patient and steady no matter what the circumstances.

Do you have that kind of patience with yourself and with others?

Christianity without love is just another what we know

cult. The world does not care
until they know that we care.

#2 Love is KIND

Just before the great Broadway star **MARY MARTIN** was to go on stage in *South Pacific*, a note was handed to her. It was from Oscar Hammerstein, one of the writers of the musical, who at that moment was on his deathbed. The short note simply said, "Dear Mary, A bell's not a bell till you ring it. **A SONG'S NOT A SONG TILL YOU SING IT**. Love in your heart is not put there to stay. **LOVE ISN'T LOVE** till you give it away."

After her stunning performance that night many people rushed backstage, crying, "Mary, what happened to you out there tonight? We never saw anything like that performance before." Blinking back the tears, Mary read them the note from Hammerstein. Then she said, "Tonight I gave my love away!"

Oscar Hammerstein was dying, but he still thought of Mary Martin and her performance. Even in his dark hour, he sought to **BRING OUT THE BEST** in someone else, and everyone who attended that performance was blessed by his kindness.

How **KIND** are you to yourself and others?

#3 Love doesn't ENVY

LOVE RELEASES; envy possesses. When you possess someone, you smother that person. If he or she fights to **GET FREE**, you try all the harder to keep control. It becomes a fight for emotional survival.

A person generally criticizes the individual whom he secretly envies—these are small attempts at **EMOTIONAL CONTROL**. The man who belittles you is probably trying to cut you down to his small self-perception. When you feel yourself turning green with envy, you're ripe for trouble. **TRUE LOVE DOES NOT ENVY!** True love is not jealous! True love is not possessive!

Does your love release your loved ones, or does it try to control them? Does your **LOVE** release yourself, or grind away at your self-esteem with past mistakes?

3

#4 Love has GOOD Manners

Management researcher and organizational expert **PETER DRUCKER** once said, "Good manners are the lubricating oil of organizations." The same is true of families, churches, or any group of people. The apostle Paul said a similar thing, "Love . . . does not behave rudely" (1 Cor. 13:4–5, NKJV).

Good manners are a way of acting so as not to offend. A mannerly person says **"PLEASE"** and **"THANK YOU"** out of love for others. A mannerly person goes to the trouble of learning and living in the basics of etiquette because that person wants to be a blessing. As a servant and ambassador of God, a follower of Christ should be the first to send a note of sympathy or **ENCOURAGEMENT**, remember birthdays and other special days, send thank you cards for gifts, use proper table manners, dress presentably at all times, and speak to others with **KINDNESS AND RESPECT**.

Good manners go before us like a herald **BRINGING GIFTS** before a king or queen arrives.

Good manners can be love's clearest voice.

#5 Love is LOYAL

DURING the Holocaust, a Polish Jewish mother with three children dashed into the woods before the approaching Nazi army. For days the mother and her children survived on roots and grass in the forest.

One morning the starving quartet was discovered by a farmer and his son, who demanded they come out of the brush. **IN AN INSTANT** the farmer saw they were starving and told his son to give the mother a loaf of bread. The mother eagerly took the loaf of bread and like a famished animal quickly broke it into three pieces. Then she **GAVE** one to each of her three children.

The farmer's son looked at his father and said, "She kept none of the bread for herself. She must not be hungry."

The Polish farmer responded, "She kept none for herself because she is a mother. She is more **LOYAL** to her children than she is to herself. Her loyalty is greater than her fear of death."

Is your love loyal?

The Key to Success . . .

Your personal definition of love

▶ _____

_____

_____

_____

_____

_____

_____

_____

_____

_____

_____

_____

_____

#6 Love is PERFUME

Of the kindnesses shown him by the Philippians, Paul said, "I am well supplied, having received from Epaphroditus the gifts you sent, a fragrant offering, a sacrifice acceptable and pleasing to God" (Phil. 4:18).

Love is perfume. Warm someone's heart today with random acts of love. Your love can be the hands of God, reshaping the self-esteem of someone crushed by cruel circumstances beyond his or her control.

There is no greater proof of God's existence than when His love flows through us to those in the world around us. Just a "whiff" of that love will change lives forever.

A **new** commandment I give to you, that you love one another: just **as I have loved** you, you also are to love one another. **By this** all people will know that you are my disciples, if you have love for one another.

—JESUS

John 13:34–35

#7 LOVE Yourself

One of the best-kept secrets of success is this: we must love ourselves before we can give love to others. If your heart is full of self-doubt and feelings of inferiority, you have nothing to give your friends, your loved ones, or those with whom you work.

The following questions can help you understand how you feel about yourself:

Do you like God?
Do you take pleasure in thinking about your future?
Do you enjoy your relationships with others?
Are you truly fond of anyone?
Would you rather be somebody else?

The only thing in the world you can change is yourself. Does your life consist of things you profess to hate, yet you continue to do them anyway? This is a betrayal of who you are. You are assassinating your self-esteem. Remember this for the rest of your life: you cannot change what you will not confront.

Are you willing to love yourself? If not, you will never fulfill what God has put you on the earth to accomplish.

FAQs

1. What are some things you feel you should change about yourself?

▸ _____

_____

_____

_____

2. What do you need to do to make these changes?

▸ _____

_____

_____

_____

3. How can you enlist God's help in making these changes and allowing more of His love to flow into and through you?

▸ _____

_____

_____

_____

What Love
IS NOT

LOVE IS NOT EMOTION.

Jesus Christ didn't say, "When I was hungry, you felt sorry for Me. When I was naked, you felt shame for Me. When I was in prison, you were embarrassed for Me. **WHEN I WAS SICK**, you were sympathetic toward Me."

His message is very clear. Love is not what you feel. **LOVE IS WHAT YOU DO.** Works, not words, are proof of your love.

LOVE IS NOT SEX.

There is sex and there is love, and you need to know the difference.

Love can lead to sex in marriage that is satisfying and meaningful, but sex outside of that **LIFE LONG COMMITMENT** will take and not give back. Sex based on lust will demand all you can give of your emotions, your time, and your material goods, while **TRUE LOVE** gives you contentment, respect, and support, both emotional and material.

Sex without that commitment can destroy your health, your mind, and your heart; **TRUE LOVE GIVES AND PROTECTS** those things instead.

journal ▶

SECRET

4

MASTERING YOUR PERSONAL ENEMY #1

There cannot be mastery of life on **any** frontier until individuals grow in the art of **mastering** themselves.

—JOHN HAGEE

A man without self-control is like a city broken into and left without walls.

—SOLOMON

Proverbs 25:28

OVER THE YEARS, I have observed the heartbreaking wreckage of lives destroyed because of the **LACK OF SELF-MASTERY**. Ministers who could shake the world with the genius of their thoughts could not, in the final analysis, control themselves. Presidents who had the ability to shape the destiny of the world fell into disgrace because of their **LACK OF SELF-CONTROL**. The majority of marriages in society and in the church end in divorce. Why? Because the discipline that could have restrained sharp words, selfish attitudes, or cruel acts in the **HEAT OF EMOTION** was totally absent.

NO MAN IS FREE WHO IS NOT MASTER OF HIMSELF.

—EPICTETUS

The degree to which a person can **CONTROL** their reactions to their emotions is the degree to which they have **MASTERY OVER THEMSELVES**.

WORRY CAN'T CHANGE THE PAST, but it can sure ruin the present and potentially your future. Worry will get you to only one place ahead of schedule: the cemetery.

There are three reasons you need to master worry:

1. Worry is faith in fear, not faith in Jesus Christ.
Worry is fear, and fear is the rejection of faith! The Bible says, "God has not given us a spirit of fear" (2 Tim. 1:7, NKJV). Fear is proof that Satan has control of your mind. Fear is evidence that you do not trust God to see you through your problem.

2. Worry is a killer.
America's finest physicians say worry is the mother of cancer, heart disease, high blood

FINALLY, brothers, whatever is true ... honorable ... excellence, if there is anything

pressure, and ulcers. It's not what you're eating sometimes as much as what's eating you.

3. Worry is useless.

Jesus said, "Which of you by worrying can add one cubit to his stature?" (Matt. 6:27, NKJV). Worry has never lifted a single burden. Worry has never solved a single problem or dried a single tear. Worry has never provided one answer for anyone, not ever.

The Antidote
TO WORRY

Do not be anxious about anything, but in everything by prayer and supplication with thanksgiving let your requests be made known to God. And the peace of God, which surpasses all understanding, will guard your hearts and your minds in Christ Jesus.

—PAUL

writing while in a Roman prison
Philippians 4:6–8

just…pure…lovely…commendable, if there is any worthy of praise, think about THESE things.

#2 the Mastery of FEAR

God gave us fear so that in a dangerous situation we would have the adrenalin to either **FIGHT OR RUN** to save our lives. God also planted the emotion of fear in our moral nature to make us uneasy with sin. Fear of the Lord, after all, is the **BEGINNING OF WISDOM**.

Satan, however, will twist fear until it **PARALYZES** us. It becomes a spirit and attitude that controls our lives. Psychiatrists describe the extremes of this spirit of fear as **PHOBIAS** that cripple our minds and our actions. It will make you look on your promised land—just

as it did for ten of the twelve Hebrew spies—and see the giants rather than the bounty God is trying to give you. It will **DECLARE THE VICTORY** of your enemies even though God is on your side.

Learn to master the **SPIRIT OF FEAR** with faith in God and His promises.

If you live in the spirit of fear, you are practicing atheism.

> **Whoever is slow to anger is better than the mighty, and he who rules his spirit than he who takes a city.** —SOLOMON
>
> Proverbs 16:32

#3 <u>the</u> MASTERY <u>of</u> Anger

Like fear, **NOT ALL ANGER IS EVIL**. Paul wrote in Ephesians 4:26, "Be angry and do not sin." Jesus said in Matthew 5:22, NKJV, "Whoever is angry with his brother *without a cause* shall be in danger of the judgment." Anger can be justified if it is just and godly. Jesus overturned the money-changers' tables in the temple with this type of just anger.

However, there are two kinds of anger that can be destructive.

1. Uncontrolled anger

When anger controls you, the outcome is never good. I've also seen a grown man kick his car because it wouldn't start. What happens when such anger shows up in a relationship? Uncontrolled anger is a destroyer.

2. Misdirected anger

What are you mad about? Are you attacking the problem or symptoms of the problem? Are you blaming others for your mistakes? Are you attacking your car or the fact that you forgot to put gas in it? Misdirected anger never leads to a solution.

#4 <u>the</u> Mastery <u>of</u> DEPRESSION

OFTEN when I am searching for a sermon series, I survey my congregation and ask them to list the major problems in their spiritual lives. On one survey I did, depression was the number one emotional problem in a congregation of eighteen thousand people. **EVEN HEROES** of faith were depressed at times.

All of us get depressed because of something from time to time, but depression that is **UNCHECKED WILL TAKE OVER** our lives and derail our hopes, dreams, and God-given purpose. We must learn how to master it, and if we cannot, we need to **ASK FOR HELP** as there may be something physically wrong we are otherwise unable to see.

Here are **SIX STEPS** to help you keep depression from conquering you.

1. Attack your problem with the power of the gospel.

2. Spend time each day meditating on God's Word.

3. Get rid of grudges daily.

4. Decide to be enthusiastic!

5. Spend time each week with committed Christians.

6. Do something nice for one special person every week.

#5 the MASTERY of Resentment

Resentment is an emotional **PRISON** built brick by brick, hurt by hurt, and tear by tear. The mind that is poisoned by resentment lives constantly in a dark world **RULED BY SUSPICION** and distrust. Those tormented souls living in the sewer of resentment are eternal victims in the unending melodrama of woe and doom and gloom.

Four Ways to Release Resentment

FIRST, ADMIT YOU ARE RESENTFUL.

You cannot change what you will not confront.

SECOND, GO TO THE PERSON WHO HAS OFFENDED YOU AND BE RECONCILED.

The cure for resentment is reconciliation. Your forgiveness will set you both free.

THIRD, STOP YOUR PITY PARTY!

Choices have consequences, and you are today what you decided yesterday to become. Stop blaming others. You are as happy or miserable as you choose to be.

FOURTH, RECOGNIZE THE IMMUTABLE SOVEREIGNTY OF GOD.

Hear this loud and clear: Nothing happens to you without God's permission, and He will never allow anything that is more than you can bear. If a situation is overcoming you, it is within your power—with His help—to fix it.

The Key to Success . . .

My first steps to self-mastery

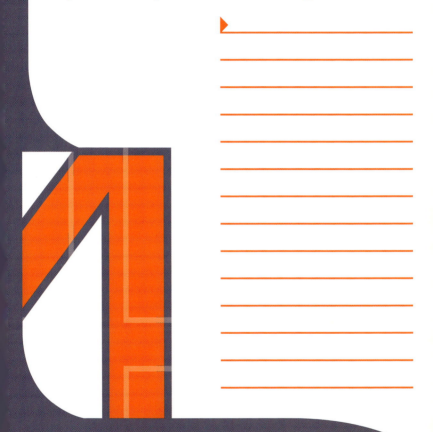

ENEMY #1

#6 the Mastery of UNFORGIVENESS

Forgiveness means **A FULL PARDON** from the pain and penalty of the past. It's a fresh start, another chance, a new beginning. **FORGIVENESS IS NOT SOFTHEARTED FOOLISHNESS**. It's a major step toward self-mastery.

Were you abused as a child? Did you cry in the night and no one came? Did your tears fall on your pillow unnoticed by anyone? Maybe you were sexually molested. There's an **INNER RAGE** known only to God and others who have been abused or sexually molested. There is **FREEDOM** through forgiveness.

DID YOU SUFFER through your parents' divorce as a child? Were you placed in an orphanage, unwanted and rejected? Did you stand alone on visitation day waiting for someone to come, and no one ever came? Are you bitter and resentful?

The list is endless, but the point is this: **THE ONLY WAY** you're ever going to have self-determination and emotional freedom is through forgiveness. **WHY?** Because until you forgive the person who hurt you, freedom is not possible. Think about it! The person you detest the most has become your master. This person is not hurting; you are. **FOR YOUR SAKE**, forgive and be free.

Forgiveness is essential to living healthy and free of burdens. **God's peace** can never come to those who refuse to forgive others.

Satan's substitute for repentance is man's rationalization of evil.

#7

the MASTERY of the Lack of REPENTANCE

There is a Bible truth most Christians simply do not grasp. That truth is this: God does not punish people for sinning; He punishes them because they refuse to *repent* of their sin.

The word **REPENT** is not a word designed in heaven to make you feel bad. The word *repent* has a very significant meaning. *Re* means **"TO RETURN."** *Pent* means **"THE HIGHEST POSITION,"** such as a penthouse or pinnacle. So the word *repent* means "to go back to the place of highest position."

Repentance is **NOT TO SHAME** you, embarrass you, or make you feel inferior or inadequate.

Repentance is designed to get you into the presence of God. There is **NO OTHER ROAD**. Repentance is the passport to renewing your relationship with God and reigniting His purpose in your life!

FAQs

1. What emotions do you feel master you from time to time?

▶

2. Are there people you harbor unforgiveness or resentment toward? What will you do about it?

▶

3. How can God help you in the area of self-mastery? What scriptures has He given you to stand on in this area?

▶

ENEMY #1

4

Do you not know that in a race all the runners compete, but only one receives the prize? So run that you may obtain it. Every athlete exercises self-control in all things. They do it to receive a perishable wreath, but we an imperishable. So I do not run aimlessly; I do not box as one beating the air. But I discipline my body and keep it under control, lest after preaching to others I myself should be disqualified.

—PAUL

1 Corinthians 9:24–27

journal ▶

ENEMY #1

SECRET

5

COMMUNICATION 101

Communication is to love and relationships what **blood** is to the body. When communication stops flowing, **you're dead**.

—JOHN HAGEE

We are rewarded
or punished
for what we say and do.

—WORDS OF WISDOM FROM THE HOLY SPIRIT
Proverbs 12:14, CEV

COMMUNICATION is an exchange of feelings or information. It takes two people to communicate—one sending, the other receiving.

The man or woman who cannot or will not communicate is alone.

If you can't communicate with the people around you, you are a **PRISONER** on an island of your own creation.

KNOW
the Five Levels

LEVEL 5: Cliché conversation

Here our **EMOTIONAL MASKS** stay on. We never reveal what we really think or feel on this shallow level. Cliché conversation goes like this: "How's your family?" The response is, "**FINE**." Yet everything around you is not fine. That kind of talk is mechanical; it's meaningless.

LEVEL 4: Reporting facts about other people

On this fourth level, we report the activities of others. The Bible calls this **GOSSIP** or tale bearing. Some people spread more filth over a telephone than you can find in a commercial vacuum cleaner.

When entertaining a conversation, measure it by these four rules:

1. Is it true?
2. Is it necessary?
3. What's my motive in telling this?
4. Will everyone involved benefit from my telling it?

If you can't answer *yes* to those four questions, **BE QUIET**.

I encourage you today to speak the and give total expression to both. It will save

<u>of</u> COMMUNICATION

Communication begins with level five, which is the least effective level of communication, and moves toward level one, which is your goal.

LEVEL 3: Sharing ideas

On this level, I will share some of the things I feel, my ideas, and some of my decisions. I will give you **JUST A PEEK** at the real me. But I will watch how you react. If you narrow your eyes, yawn, or look at your watch, I will not continue communicating at this level. I will go back to level four or five where my speech is totally superficial.

Remember, communication is a **TWO-WAY PROCESS**. I will open to you, but I will expect your input—verbal or non verbal.

LEVEL 2: Reveal real feelings and emotions

Level two is **GUT-LEVEL** conversation. This is what I feel deep in my soul. Level two communication has no fear of a blow up, pouting, or resentment because of a petty disagreement.

LEVEL 1: Peak communication

Level one is two human beings in absolute honesty. There is no pretense here. There is **ABSOLUTE TRANSPARENCY** because I am not trying to hide any detail of my life from you. When you hide behind a mask in pretense of being what you never can be, **REAL COMMUNICATION** will never happen.

unspeakable, think the unthinkable, your relationships and your sanity.

#2 FOUR Enemies of COMMUNICATION

In order to communicate effectively—whether it's speech class or in the boardroom—learn to avoid these enemies that will kill any chance of success.

1. DISCLAIMERS

Some people use tag phrases so that others will buy into their agenda, but using them can make you appear to be unsure of yourself. Saying things like:

You may not like this, but...

I may be wrong about this, but...

This may be a stupid question, but...

Disclaimers not only diminish your credibility but also dramatically decrease your level of influence and invites listeners to disagree with you and not take you seriously.

2. FILLERS

Any speech instructor will tell you to avoid fillers like "um," "well," "uh," "y'know." This signals you're uncertain about what you're saying and that you came unprepared. It also opens the door for someone to interrupt you.

3. RAMBLING

Women, more than men, tend to ramble. They add too many details instead of getting to the point. Don't overwhelm your listener with details. Instead, get to the central point of your idea first and hit it hard.

4. NOT KNOWING HOW OR WHEN TO CHOOSE YOUR BATTLES

There is wisdom in waiting to bring up issues or problems. Many times these things will take care of themselves. Make sure you have all the facts before you jump in.

102

Adapted from *What Queen Esther Knew* by Connie Glaser and Barbara Smalley

#3 LISTEN <u>for</u> GOD'S Communication

When God speaks, do you hear? God is constantly trying to speak to us, but the question is: Are we listening?

God spoke to Samuel, Moses, and Abraham. He talked with Adam and Eve **FACE-TO-FACE**. "OK," you say, "God spoke to those biblical people, but He doesn't speak to me." Let me correct you there. God does speak to you today in different ways.

FIRST, God speaks plainly and powerfully through the Bible. The Old Testament gives us His direction for His people, the Israelites, and for us. And the New Testament reveals **THE TRUTH** of His Son's direction for our lives.

SECOND, God communicates to humanity through nature. Nature is God's billboard for the past and God's billboard for tomorrow.

#4 LISTEN to YOUR Conscience

Your conscience is a God-given instrument that allows you to determine right from wrong. Conscience is the lamp of God saying, "This is the way, walk in it." Conscience is the compass of the soul.

THANK GOD for your conscience. Before radar, before sonar, before the compass, God provided every man this built-in navigational direction finder. Ignore your conscience, and you will destroy your soul, your peace of mind, your family, your career, and eventually your eternal soul. How does your conscience affect your communication? Let me give you this illustration.

You hear that your boss has maligned you and questioned your ability. Your flesh says, "I'm hurt. I've been offended!"

Your mind says, "This is a personal attack. I should get angry and resign immediately."

Your conscience thunders back as the spiritual voice of heaven, "**BLESSED ARE YOU** when they revile you and persecute you, and say all kinds of evil against you falsely...Rejoice and be exceedingly glad, for great is your reward in heaven" (Matt. 5:11–12, NKJV).

WHAT ATTITUDE WILL YOU CHOOSE? Are you going to be a victor or a victim? Trials must surrender to triumph if you **LISTEN** to your conscience.

#5

BEWARE of
Communication
Killers

Five communication killers that will destroy every attempt you make to communicate effectively are:

1. The fear of rejection

2. Lack of honesty

3. An explosive response

4. Tears

5. Silence

The Key to Success . . .

My first step to effective communication

#6 Be OPEN to YOUR Imagination

When I gave marriage counseling, I used what I called the "Ezekiel method of communication." This is communication through imagination.

Ezekiel was the preacher in a concentration camp of Jews exiled in Babylon. These Jews were **SLAVES AND REFUGEES** of war who had lost their homes, their freedom, and their hope. Ezekiel wanted to communicate with them, so God told him to go down and "sit where they sit."

So Ezekiel became a **CAPTIVE**. He let the blows of humiliation that fell on their backs fall on his back. He looked at the world through their eyes and felt what they felt.

A CLASSIC PRAYER says, "Lord, help me never to judge another man until I have walked in his moccasins for two weeks." Ezekiel did exactly that. Most people will not listen to someone who has not experienced what they have.

Always be open to letting your imagination help you understand another person's perspective.

To share a moment of suffering or sorrow in silent compassion is **REAL COMMUNICATION.**

COMPASSION is a result of your relationship with God.

#7
SPEAK <u>the</u> Truth <u>in</u> LOVE

Paul told the Ephesians, "Speak the truth in love" (Eph. 4:15, NLT). The more truth you speak, the more love you should convey.

Truth is a two-edged sword. Be very careful when you approach someone with it. In order to speak the truth in love, be sure to plan a good time for communication with that person. In the Hagee household, I wake up at 6:00 a.m. and explode out of bed with enough energy to hurt myself. Diana doesn't warm up until about 9:00 a.m. We don't talk much in the mornings. When she gets up and gets in high gear, she can move mountains—but it won't happen early.

Then allow for a reaction time. Remember, you have had the advantage of thinking about what you are going to say. You have prepared your case as cleverly and thoroughly as the famous courtroom attorney Clarence Darrow. Don't be amazed if he or she thinks about your conversation for a day or two and comes back with a whole new response.

FAQs

1. Which communication killers are holding you back? List them.

▶ _____

_____

_____

_____

2. When was the last time you heard from God? What did He say to you?

▶ _____

_____

_____

_____

3. If a friend is going through a difficult time, do you just listen and let the friend talk, or do you feel you have to say something? Why?

▶ _____

_____

_____

_____

COMM 101

5

He who has ears to hear, let him hear!

—GOD
Matthew 11:15

journal ▶

SECRET

6

PLUGGING INTO THE POWER SOURCE

The **tragedy** of our day is not unanswered prayer, but **unoffered** prayer. Unfortunately, the situation is desperate, but the church **is not**.

—JOHN HAGEE

First of all, then, I urge that supplications, prayers, intercessions, and thanksgivings be made for all people, for kings and **all** who are in high positions, that we may lead a peaceful and quiet life, godly and dignified **in every way.**

—PAUL

1 Timothy 2:1–2

Here is one of my mother's favorite statements about prayer:

SOME PRAYER; SOME POWER.
MORE PRAYER; MORE POWER.
MUCH PRAYER; MUCH POWER.

The question each of us must ask is this: how much power do I want from God? **YOUR ANSWER** is probably very simple: lots. Yet we have as much or as little of God's power **RIGHT NOW** as we are willing to pray to receive.

A prayerless Christian is a powerless Christian.

But a prayerful Christian can accomplish **ANYTHING**—even change the course of a nation.

#1 PRAYER

Should be Your FIRST CHOICE not Your LAST CHANCE

I can recall countless times when **DISTRESSED SOULS** walked into my office telling the most heartrending stories, and then pleading, "Please, let's do something about this."

When I say, "**LET'S PRAY** about this together," invariably they look at me in frustration and say, "I really want to **DO SOMETHING** about this!"

Let me tell you, you're not doing anything worthwhile about your problem until you **BEGIN PRAYING** about it.

#2 PRAYER Prepares YOU to do God's WILL

When Saul, **THE PHARISEE**, was strutting down the Damascus road, threatening the New Testament church, God looked over the balconies of heaven at this brilliant, opinionated, **TYPE-A**, hard-charging crusader and said, "That's my man!"

God stripped Saul of his religious arrogance and **BLINDED** him with a bright light from heaven. Scripture tells us, "For three days he was without sight, and neither ate nor drank" (Acts 9:9). Those three days in darkness were saturated with soul-searching prayer that God answered by telling Ananias, **"RISE AND GO** to the street called Straight, and at the house of Judas look for a man of Tarsus named Saul, for behold, *he is praying*" (Acts 9:11, emphasis added).

Saul's prayer was not getting God ready to do Saul's will—which was to put Christians in prison—Saul's prayer prepared Saul to **DO GOD'S WILL**.

Does God have you **IN A DARK PLACE**? Seek His face with a pure heart, and His light will break through. **PRAYER IS THE GATEWAY** to God's will being done on earth, and doing God's will is the gateway to gaining His favor!

#3 Pray SCRIPTURE

WHAT IS YOUR PROBLEM?

Your burden? Your crisis? Find the verses in the Bible that relate to what you're going through and pray those verses. (In the beginning you might need to consult a concordance. You might look up the word **WORRY**, for instance, and then look for the passages that apply to overcoming it.) Remember, it's not the problem you're going *through*; it's God's

SOLUTION you're going *to* that counts.

We pray Scripture to remind God of His promises in the Bible and also to remind ourselves of those promises so we can latch onto them with our faith. **OBVIOUSLY** we cannot pray Scripture unless we know Scripture. Get into God's Word daily so you can pray Scripture **WITH POWER**.

#4 Consider the POWER of Two

Jesus said to His church, "Whatever you bind on earth will be bound in heaven... Again I say to you that if two of you agree on earth concerning anything that they ask, it will be done for them by My Father in heaven" (Matt. 18:18–19, NKJV).

Two in agreement can do **MORE** than two million in discord.

The message is very clear. The initiative rests with us, not God! **STOP ASKING**, "When is God going to do something about my situation?" God has placed the responsibility of taking action squarely on our shoulders. **START PRAYING** in Jesus' name in agreement with another believer, and watch for powerful results.

What area of your life is **UNDER ATTACK**? Your relationships? Your job? Your finances? Your health? Your emotions?

Find someone with whom you can **AGREE** right now. If you take the initiative, the power unleashed by your prayer of agreement will move heaven to bring the perfect answer.

> **Jesus did not teach His disciples how to preach, but He did teach them how to pray.**

#5 PRAY in the Spirit

God's **SECRET WEAPON** in prayer is praying in the Spirit. The apostle Paul writes:

> Likewise the Spirit helps us in our weakness. For we do not know what to pray for as we ought, but the Spirit himself intercedes for us with groanings too deep for words. And he who searches hearts knows what is the mind of the Spirit, because the Spirit intercedes for the saints according to the will of God.
>
> —ROMANS 8:26–27

Note that our **WEAKNESS** in this verse is in our minds. We do not know what we should pray for. We have a language barrier with heaven; therefore, the Holy Spirit makes **INTERCESSION** to God in heaven for us, saying, "Father, here is what Your child is trying to say."

Praying in the Spirit helps you **HIT THE BULL'S-EYE** every time you get on your knees.

The Key to Success . . .

My prayer plan

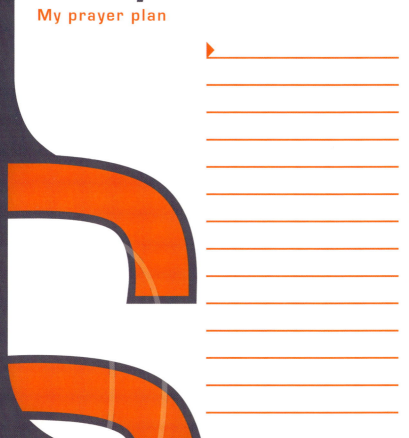

▶ _____

_____

_____

_____

_____

_____

_____

_____

_____

_____

_____

_____

_____

_____

_____

#6 Prayer GIVES YOU the POWER to Shape the DESTINY of NATIONS

In 701 B.C., King Sennacherib of Assyria marched his legions toward **JERUSALEM** for the purpose of slaughtering the Jews. Once he arrived outside the city, Sennacherib sent a message to King Hezekiah, promising to slaughter every citizen of Jerusalem the next morning. Terrified, Hezekiah pulled out his **SECRET WEAPON**: prayer. He laid Sennacherib's letter before the Lord and said, "Look what this heathen has written to You, O God." (See Isaiah 37:14.)

The next morning when Hezekiah looked over the fortified walls of the city of Jerusalem by the dawn's early light, he saw **185,000** Assyrians were dead. Hezekiah prayed, and the destiny of his nation was **CHANGED**.

Intoxicated with unbroken success, we have become **too self-sufficient** to feel the necessity of redeeming and preserving grace, **too proud** to pray to the God that made us! It behooves us, then, to **humble** ourselves before the offended Power, to **confess** our national sins, and to **pray** for clemency and forgiveness.

—ABRAHAM LINCOLN

in his declaration "For a Day of National Humiliation, Fasting, and Prayer" in response to the Civil War

#7

Prayer <u>is</u> a WEAPON God <u>has</u> GIVEN <u>to</u> Wage WAR <u>in</u> <u>the</u> HEAVENLIES

Prayer and praise can be offensive weapons in the war against evil. The enemy is Satan and his kingdom. Prayer and praise give strength to the body of Christ to conquer darkness in any form. Praise combined with the Word of God is an instrument of justice.

Paul wrote in 1 Corinthians 6:2–3: "Do you not know that the saints will judge the world? ...Do you not know that we are to judge angels?" We have power through prayer and praise to bring judgment against evil powers and principalities and to release God's will on the earth.

Praise gives strength to the body of Christ to conquer the prince of darkness.

FAQs

1. What are areas in your community that you feel need regular prayer?

2. What are areas in your personal life you should pray for every day?

3. What are the things God has put on your heart to remember and intercede for when you pray?

The Only Seven Scriptural REASONS
God Doesn't Answer Prayer

1. We do not ask.
2. We do not pray in Jesus' name.
3. We do not ask according to God's will.
4. We do not pray in faith believing.
5. We do not pray specifically.
6. We do not remove unconfessed sin.
7. We do not forgive.

Pray without ceasing.

—PAUL

1 Thessalonians 5:17

journal ▶

The **difference** between the wealthy and the poor is this: **The wealthy invest their money** and spend what's left; the poor spend their money and invest what's left. . . . When what you have in your hands is **not enough** to meet your need, what you have in your hands is your seed. **Prosperity** begins with investing in God's will and work.

—JOHN HAGEE

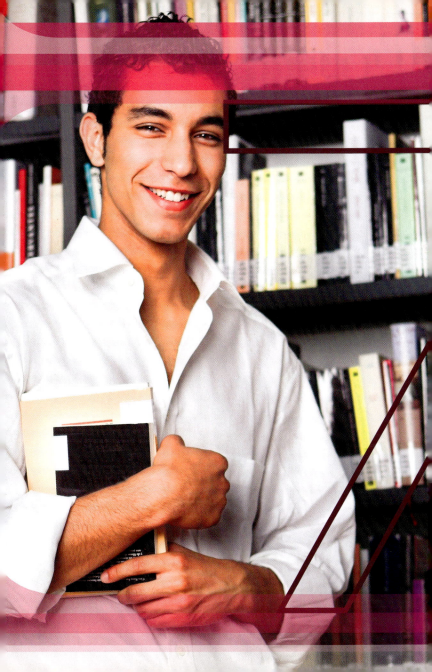

One who is faithful in a very little is also faithful in much, and one who is dishonest in a very little is also dishonest in much. If then you have not been faithful in the unrighteous wealth, who will entrust to you the true riches?... No servant can serve two masters.... You cannot serve God and money.

—JESUS

Luke 16:10–11, 13

JESUS CHRIST gave us thirty-eight parables. Sixteen of those thirty-eight parables deal with managing money.

More is said in the New Testament about **MANAGING YOUR MONEY** than about heaven and hell combined. Five times more is said about money than prayer. While there are five hundred plus verses on both prayer and faith, over two thousand verses deal with money and your possessions.

Think about that.

THE BIBLE IS THE GREATEST FINANCIAL MANUAL EVER PRINTED.

God's Word makes it clear that you will either **MASTER YOUR MONEY**, or your money will master you.

Principles of
INVESTMENT

A wise minister I know advises, "Sow to the **FUTURE**, reap from the past." For him, mastering money is all about investing. When you invest, you don't just throw your money at things, but wisely sow it into what is good and profitable. Always invest in the future first. Then when those investments **PAY OFF**, there will be plenty to buy whatever you **NEED OR WANT**.

The Bible calls us **STEWARDS** because everything really belongs to God. He has provided it to take care of ourselves and our families, as well as expand His kingdom on the earth. Look at the following **SEVEN LAWS** for investing what God has entrusted to you. When you faithfully observe these seven undeniable laws of investment, the power of **GOD'S ABUNDANCE** will be unleashed in your life.

#1 Invest in YOURSELF

There are two words that keep many Christians from succeeding. Those two words are *self-interest* and *selfishness*. Too many Christians think their definitions are the same.

A quick look at *Webster's Ninth New Collegiate Dictionary* tells us that **SELF-INTEREST** means "a concern for one's own advantage and well-being"; whereas **SELFISH** is defined as "concerned excessively or exclusively with oneself; seeking or concentrating on one's own advantage, pleasure, or well-being without regard for others."

Jesus taught us to **INVEST WISELY** by investing in things that are permanent. "It's not in your self-interest," He said, "to invest in something that moths can eat, or rust can decay, or thieves can carry off, or the IRS can tax out of existence; store up your money in heaven instead" [Matt. 6:19–20, HIT].

Invest in **YOURSELF** by investing in the kingdom of God. Lay up for yourself treasures in heaven, because the kingdom of God is **THE ONLY CERTAIN INVESTMENT OPPORTUNITY** you have. Wall Street will collapse, the economy of America will eventually fold, but the kingdom of God will stand **FOREVER**.

#2 Invest in OTHERS

This is an undeniable law of prosperity: "givers gain." God has created a universe where it is impossible to receive without giving.

GOD ALMIGHTY CONTROLS the economy of the world, and He controls your income. The United States government is not your source; God is. The stock market is not your source; **GOD IS**. Your IRA account is not your source; **GOD IS**. Your rich aunt is not your source; **GOD IS**. Deuteronomy 8:18 says, "Remember the LORD your God, for it is he who gives you power to get wealth."

"Give, and it will be given to you" (Luke 6:38) is the law of God. Until you give, you don't **QUALIFY** to receive God's power to get wealth.

In God's economy there is no such thing as a "fixed income." Your income is **CONTROLLED BY YOUR GIVING**.

#3 Qualifiers <u>for</u> GOD'S ABUNDANCE

1. **Be His child:** How do you expect to inherit something from God if you are not in His family?

2. **Tithe**: The first 10 percent of anything you make is God's. If you are not faithful with that small amount, how do you expect Him to trust you with more?

3. **Work hard and well**: Be diligent in your work, as if whatever you do is for the Lord and not just people.

4. **Stay out of debt**: The average cost of something purchased with a credit card not paid off at the end of each month is 112 percent higher than if you had paid cash. Save and wait instead.

5. **Have a plan for your future and your business**: Most people don't plan to fail, but failing to plan is really the same thing!

6. **Don't partner with unbelievers**: God doesn't want to enrich the devil's crowd with your inheritance.

7. **Do not let the spirit of fear steal God's blessings**: When opportunity knocks, send faith and wisdom to answer, and lock fear in the closet!

#4

1. Give the treasure of your time.

The greatest gift you can give others is your time. Make sure you give more to them than you do to the television or other time wasters.

2. Be a promise keeper.

When you tell someone you're going to do something, do it. Don't make excuses; simply do it.

3. Get rest.

Psychologists are now saying that American marriages are stressed due to tension from overwork and lack of rest. Take time to relax so that you can be the best for God, your friends, and your family.

4. Build a family creed based on faith in God.

MANAGE *your* Greatest ASSETS

Your greatest assets are your relationships, particularly those involving the spouse and children you will one day have. I suggest the following eight essential keys to help you cherish them properly.

When you as a parent pray with your children each night, they see you put God first. When your children see you give the first fruits of your labor to the church, they see you put God first. That attitude will carry over. Start putting God first now, long before you start a family.

5. Manage your time.

Every person wakes up every day with the same amount of time; the difference in their success or failure is in how they use it. Manage your time to accomplish important things, not just keeping busy.

6. Learn to say no.

One of the most powerful and eloquent words in the English language is *no*. This single word can save your time, your money, your relationships, your health, and your sanity.

7. Bless your children.

Bless your children on a regular basis. Release the anointing of God into their lives to accomplish the divine destiny God has for each of them.

8. Work at staying physically fit.

It's your future; be there for it. Take care of the physical body God gave you because it is also a treasure. You will not recognize the value of your health until you lose it—but I suggest putting that off as long as possible.

#5

BE Patient in WAITING for Your Prosperity

Everything God does on earth comes from the principle of seedtime and harvest. Genesis 8:22 says, "While the earth remains, seedtime and harvest...shall not cease." If you plant your seed today, and then keep digging it up to see if it has grown, harvest will never come!

You can plant your seed properly and abundantly in **GOOD GROUND**, but you can ki!l your harvest with a **LACK OF PATIENCE**. Esau sold his birthright for a bowl of pottage because of his impatience. He saw the bowl of pottage his brother, Jacob, had made and said, "I am about to die; of what use is a birthright to me?" (Gen. 25:32). He wasn't anywhere close to death, but his impatience destroyed his inheritance.

If you invest a dollar—or a hundred or a thousand—in the kingdom of God today, don't look for a hundredfold return **BEFORE THE SUN SETS**. If you will be patient, **GOD WILL MULTIPLY** your seed beyond your needs.

The Key to Success . . .

My investment plan

▶ _____

_____

_____

_____

_____

_____

_____

_____

_____

_____

_____

_____

_____

_____

#6 CONQUER the Poverty COMPLEX

Some of God's children have a poverty complex. It sounds like this: "Jesus was poor. I'm poor. I'm like Jesus." That's absolutely wrong.

THE BIBLE does say in 2 Corinthians 8 that Christ "for your sakes became poor," but the question must be asked, when did He become poor? The answer is this: He became poor at **THE CROSS** when He took my poverty.

While He walked on the earth, Jesus always had more than enough—from the expensive gifts He received from the wise men to the fine clothes the Roman soldiers fought over at his crucifixion. Jesus **NEVER** had a poverty complex—He always had more than enough—and if we are to be like Him, we must reject the "I don't have **ENOUGH**" complex as well. God can do miracles with what little you have if you **TRUST HIM** with it and follow His instructions.

God doesn't care how many **things** you own as long as those things do not own you.... If you will **invest in winning the lost**, God will give you abundance you cannot contain.

—JOHN HAGEE

#7 God GIVES WEALTH to Those Who PASS the Blessing ON

God does not have trouble getting money to us; He has trouble getting money through us. God said to Abraham, "I will bless you...so that you will be a blessing" (Gen. 12:2).

ABRAHAM is our spiritual father. Galatians 3:29 states, "If you are Christ's, then you are Abraham's offspring, **HEIRS** according to promise." Abraham was a mighty man of wealth, and God used that wealth to birth the nation of Israel.

How can people come to know God today without a preacher? And how can preachers be sent out unless someone has the abundance to send them? **NOT ONE** missionary can be sent and not one church can be built without someone having **MORE THAN ENOUGH** to take care of themselves and their families. Not one television program or telecast can be made without abundance.

God's abundance is to be used to teach the gospel because every man and woman, every boy and girl without Christ will spend eternity in hell. **WINNING THE LOST** is God's top priority, and if you will invest in winning the lost, God will **GIVE** you abundance you cannot contain.

FAQs

1. For every dollar you receive, how many cents, on average, do you give to God? How many do you sow into your future? Put away for possible emergencies? Spend on yourself?

▶ _____

_____

_____

_____

2. How do you think God would want you to adjust the spending pattern you just described?

▶ _____

_____

_____

_____

7

God is able **to make all grace abound to you, so that having all sufficiency** in all things **at all times, you may abound in** every **good work.**

—PAUL
2 Corinthians 9:8

journal ▶

OVERFLOW